Alaska's Secret Door

By Judy Ferguson

Illustrated by Nikola Kocic

My name is Clint...

I live with Dad and Mom on the Tanana, a glacial river
in Alaska. From our house on a hill, I can see the
Tanana, the Alaska Range and eagles soaring on the wind.
Can you see my secret window next to me? It is my loft. I like
to sit with my best friend, Jessica, on the roof of our house and
watch the boats go by.

In the spring when I was five, I carved a boat
from the bark of a cottonwood tree.
Dad and I walked to the bank of the rushing river.
Together, we pushed my toy canoe into the Tanana, foaming with
spring's melted snow.
The current caught the light craft and I watched my canoe bounce on
the swirling water... Dad said, "toward the sea..."
At the house, Dad pointed to a map, "In parts of Alaska," he said, "the
rivers are the only roads." He added, "Clint, let's follow the water trail.
We'll pack our big canoe and see what your little boat will see!"

On June 21st, when the Arctic summer sun
never sets, Mom got into our 19-foot canoe;
then I scrambled in the middle. Dad climbed
in behind me and pulled on the motor's cord.
When we pushed out, the startled geese
sunning on the sandbar flew away. Our
canoe rode up the river swells and then
...sloop! down the other side.
We passed two moose when suddenly the
channel became shallow. Our motor dug into
the river bottom! Dad jumped in the
freezing water and pulled; Mom slipped out
and pushed! I stayed safe and dry. And,
finally, we were free! On the way to
Fairbanks, I got hungry. Mom made me a
sandwich on a paddle, then she served it
beneath my nose.

The Midnight Sun bathed the sand with gold as we tied the boat
for the night. Dad made a fire while I fished for Northern Pike.
(I wondered if my toy canoe might be inside the fish tugging
on my line... (?!))
Mom cleaned the slimy creature on a log, and said, "Pikes' teeth
are sharp!" (I looked inside the fish, and there was no toy boat!)
We ate fried fish by the flickering flames. Across the river, we saw
the road to Nenana winding up a hill. "From that town," Dad said,
"the river trail to the Bush begins. There, the Demientieff Barge
gets its goods: trucks, bikes and flour to carry to the villagers on
the Yukon River and to the sea."

As we loaded the canoe the next day, the sternwheeler that tourists ride, passed with its paddles churning in the muddy water. (I hoped my canoe didn't get caught in that eggbeater!) In the tent that night, Dad warned, "Tomorrow we face Squaw Crossing. It's open water we have to cross before we enter the Yukon River. If there's wind, the waves get very big..." Mom's face looked white.

As I lay in my sleeping bag, I wondered if my little boat had made it through those waves.
The next morning, we motored our canoe close to shore, praying. With no wind, Squaw Crossing was as smooth as glass. Around the curve, we came to the end of our home river, the Tanana. (I hoped my little boat had made that turn!)

When we looked upstream -- we gasped. The mighty
Yukon River was curving toward us, carrying the waters
of Canada. It touched the village of Tanana then flowed
across Alaska to the Bering Sea. Mom said, "Here, in old
times, Native Alaskans gathered at 'Nu-chuh-luh-woy-uh:'
meaning, 'Between the Rivers,' to trade."
In our big canoe, we entered the Yukon's sweeping waters.
I was happy ... we still might catch my little canoe ...

On our first night camped on the majestic Yukon -- just across from Tanana -- a full moon showed against a blue evening sky. While Dad and I lay in our bags, listening to wolves howl, Mom sat outside the tent. I heard her whisper, "I didn't know there was a back door, a secret door ... to a hidden Alaska ... of sand, river, sun and salmon."

On the banks of the village of Tanana, kids with bikes met our canoe. They invited me to hop
on and take a ride!

In the bright sunshine, Kathleen peeled sweet willow branches. She gave them to all
the bike gang kids -- hmm -- village candy!

But no one there had seen my cottonwood canoe bouncing on the waves.

As we continued down the river, I craned my neck looking for my boat,
but instead -- around the bend -- there was another village, this
one seemed to slide into the river; it was Ruby!

When we docked, Doo-Doo offered me a ride on his bike. We rode up the steep road past the old roadhouse. While we were gone, Dad and Mom saw Emmitt Peters, the winner of the 1000-mile, Iditarod Dogsled Race, wearing a baseball cap and dark glasses, sitting on the post office steps. Doo-Doo and I rode up to Emmitt; he let me pet his lead dog, Nugget. Together, they had mushed from Anchorage to Nome that year -- 1975 -- in 14 days, 14 hours and 43 minutes: the fastest ever!

He invited us to his parents' fish camp the next day. It began to rain. Through the droplets, the glow of the Midnight Sun colored Ruby with a rosy wash. Suddenly, the barge horn blew, "Th-wonkkkkk." At midnight, people rushed to Demientieff's barge to get their bikes, trucks and flour.

The next day, we canoed to the Peters' fish camp. Emmitt had chained his record-setting dog team at the base of the old telegraph station, now Mary and Paul Peters' cabin. Racks of chum salmon hung drying in the wind for dog food.

The Peters' grandchildren, Timmy, Nina and Philip, were catching whitefish fry down by the river with a toy fish wheel! But no one had trapped my little canoe.

Sweet alder smoke curled from a tent near the cabin. Inside, moose hides and fish were drying in the smoke. Mary opened the tent flaps, took some salmon strips, and slipped them in a skillet in the small oven of her wood stove. Rich, oily juice began to pool in the pan. 'Eyuga,' she called the dish as she piled the thick salmon bacon onto an overflowing platter.

Setting ten plates on her table, Mary noticed Norman from Ruby approaching. Mary confided, "Norman came so he can eat Native food: smoked salmon, pilot bread, and coffee." "Hm-m-m good," Mom said. I loaded the dripping fish on my cracker and munched!

After lunch, Timmy slammed open the cabin door, and cried, "The salmon are running!!" Emmitt ran for the shore. The fish wheel's baskets were spinning in the current, flipping slithering salmon into the waiting fish box.

Had my toy boat landed in a basket? I couldn't see it! We said, "Good-bye" to Emmitt's family and headed for Nulato where, Mom said, "Russians used to live in the early days."

When we docked at the village of Nulato, we were greeted by two giggling girls, Shirley and Cecelia. We walked uphill with them to the cemetery, overlooking the river. On that high bluff, I searched for my toy canoe in the wide river but I only saw waves. Shirley, Cecelia and I ran and hid from each other in the tall grass between the graves, stuffing warm blueberries in our mouths.

As the sun began to set, Mom read the names on the markers. She explained, "When Alaska was owned by Russia, the Cossacks came up the Yukon River as far as Nulato. Now only their names remain on the white crosses."

The sun shone on the river as we left Nulato. After passing several villages, mom and dad decided to leave the Yukon to go up the Innoko River to the isolated village of Shageluk. We turned our canoe into the Yukon's four-foot, roller waves. White-knuckled, Mom held onto the boat's sides. Dad gunned the 6-horsepower motor up the waves, and then let off in the valleys: Brr-Up! down ... Up again! I felt very small! (But my dad was driving the boat!) Finally, we turned into the quiet Innoko River. On the hillside, a bear was eating blueberries. In front of us, a tugboat was pushing a small barge. Steering the boat from the pilot house, Claude Demientieff waved to us.

As evening shadows covered the Innoko, we were still boating around the river bends. Mom and I began to sing, "I'm tired; I'm hungry and I'm cold...; but my man just goes on and on!"

When we finally made camp, I saw the Demientieff barge parked across the river for the night.

The next morning when we walked into Shageluk, the people were so shy. Inside their log homes, children peeked at us from behind their curtains. Lucy Hamilton, an elder, met us by the riverbank carrying a cup of agutak: moose fat blended with blueberries, cooked salmon and sugar -- Native ice cream! We stuck our fingers in--Yum! The village chief, Adolph Hamilton, took Dad, Mom, and me to the old kazheem, the community sweat bath, where the shaman once held mask dances. "At Shageluk," Adolph told us, "we are between Athabascan Indian and Yupik Eskimo lands."

The Demientieff Barge finally pulled up at Shageluk.
Claude Demientieff walked toward me, carrying a piece of
wood... (I wondered, "Could it be...?") He began, "Young man,
I found this in a log jam on the Yukon two nights ago. Could
this be yours...?" In his big warm hand, he held -- all muddy,
droopy, and wet -- my cottonwood bark canoe!! Mom and Dad
thought we'd never see it again ... but I knew we would!
I had been looking (through Alaska's secret door...)

I held my boat tightly. Dad smiled, "Perfect! The geese
are flying! Berries are ripe! Summer's over; winter's
coming! Your toy boat will lead us home, but -- this
time -- in your arms!" Silhouetted against the sunset,
Lucy and Adolph waved good-bye as we pushed off.
"Good-bye, mighty Yuke!"we called, and turned our canoe
upstream, leaving a land never dreamed of, returning home
on the water trail -- back through -- Alaska's Secret Door.

Glossary

Agutak/Native Ice Cream
To boiled fish, add three dips of melted game tallow, add sugar and berries, mix with snow or cottonwood fluff.

Russian-America
The name for Alaska when it belonged to Russia before 1867.

Glacial-fed River
A river formed from melting glaciers, and silt, a dirt powder, resulting in opaque water.

Pilot Bread
A heavy, round cracker: light to pack, stores well, substitutes for bread.

Athabascan
The aboriginal Indians of the Alaskan and Canadian Interior.

Fishwheel
A device in which two paddle-like spokes holding two wire baskets scoop returning adult salmon. The river current pushes the paddles that rotate on a wooden axle. The fish fall live into a holding box. The people cut the fish for drying, providing the Athabascan people with fish for winter.

Kazheem
Derived from Central Yup'ik qasgiq of Southwest Alaska: a men's gathering place/sweat bath where the local shaman held mask dances.

Shaman
An individual who interceded over the power of evil spirits. The practice weakened in the late 1800's.

Sternwheeler
A boat powered by a paddle mounted on the back of the craft, driven by steam or by fuel.

Midnight Sun
Between May-July, the sun in the far North shines many hours; it never sets on June 21st.

Smoke-tanned Moosehide
A mooseskin that has been hand-processed and smoked until it is like cloth. In 1975 when Mary Peters was 60 years old, she had tanned 65 moosehides by hand.

Yupik Eskimo
The aboriginal people who generally live in coastal, Southwest Alaska.

For Martha Eskridge; my mother, who believed in this book; for Clint on his 34th birthday; for his children, Hunter and Halle; for Reb, Sarah and Ben; and, for the children of the world. J.F.

For Ema. N.K.

We welcome reader response: Glas Publishing: 907 895 4101; outpost@wildak.net; Box 130, Delta Junction, Alaska 99737.

Author, Judy Ferguson; husband, Reb and 5-year-old Clint, Yukon River, 1975.

Emmitt Peters, the winner of the 1000-mile, Iditarod Dogsled Race and lead dog, Nugget, 1975.

Paul, Timmy, Mary, Nina, Philip Peters, Melozi Fishcamp, Ruby, Alaska, 1975.

Thanks to Dragan Miskovic and Rastko Ciric for recommending Nikola Kocic; salute to Predrag Dencic, Milorad Latovljev and Dusan Vojnov; and, to Publikum.
Layout: Dragan Miskovic.
Proofreaders: Marian Sexton, Joyce McCombs, Diana Harper. Maps: Nikola Kocic and Diane Folaron.
April 2004. Alaska's Secret Door
Text Copyright©2004 Judy Ferguson
Illustrations copyright©2004 Nikola Kocic
Printed in Belgrade, Serbia-Montenegro, Publikum Printing.

First Paperback edition, April 2004.
Library of Congress Cataloguing-in-Publication Data
Printed in Belgrade, Serbia-Montenegro, Publikum Printing.

Illustrator, Nikola Kocic, Belgrade, Serbia-Montenegro, 2004. nkocic@eunet.yu; 011 381 18 327 582; Bulevar Nemanjica 76/69, Nis, Serbia-Montenegro (Former Yugoslavia)